rubber STAMP extravaganza

rubber STAMP extravaganza

Vesta Abel

NORTH LIGHT BOOKS
CINCINNATI, OHIO

about the author

I was fortunate enough to be born to creative parents who introduced me to a wonderful world of travel, art, home schooling, philosophy and an incredible array of interesting friends. They were amazing role models who kept me supplied with art materials and interesting travel locations, often at great sacrifice to themselves. All of these things influenced the person I am today, and I am grateful for this opportunity to say thank you. I hope I will always make you proud of your efforts.

In 1980 I cofounded Comotion rubber stamps; I am also founder of ArtSeeds.com, whose mission is to scatter the seeds of creativity to all who are interested.

Rubber Stamp Extravaganza. © 2001 by Vesta Abel. Manufactured in China. All rights reserved. No part of this book may be reproduced in any form or by any electronic or mechanical means including information storage and retrieval systems without permission in writing from the publisher, except by a reviewer, who may quote brief passages in review. Published by North Light Books, an imprint of F&W Publications, Inc., 1507 Dana Avenue, Cincinnati, Ohio 45207. (800) 289-0963. First edition.

Other fine North Light Books are available from your local bookstore, art supply store or direct from the publisher.

05 04 03 02 01   5 4 3 2 1

Library of Congress Cataloging-in-Publication Data
Abel, Vesta (Vesta Iris)
   Rubber stamp extravaganza / by Vesta Abel
      p. cm.
   Includes index.
   ISBN 1-58180-128-9 (alk. paper)
   1. Rubber stamp printing. I. Title.

TT867 .A26 2001
761--dc21   00-048067

Editor: Jane Friedman
Designer: Andrea Short
Layout Artist: Kathy Bergstrom
Production Coordinator: Sara Dumford
Photographers: Al Parrish and Christine Polomsky
Photo Stylist: Jan Nickum

introduction

Have you ever wished you were artistic but felt you were not blessed with the ability to create beautiful works of art? Well, hopefully by reading this book you will awaken that creative spirit, which we all possess.

This book shows you easy step-by-step instructions on how to create not only practical home decor projects, but also beautiful cards, jewelry, candles, book covers and more.

Stamps have been around and used since ancient times; whether they are made of wood, metal, stone or rubber, they all achieve wonderful effects. They help us become "instant artists" with the use of other crafting materials.

We live in a wonderful age when we have access to amazing products, such as embossing powders, specialty inks, foams, veneers, shrink plastics, clays, glues, metals and more.

Are you ready to go on a wonderful journey of artistic self-expression, fun and adventure? If the spirit is willing, follow me. . . . . .

Tools & Materials

Rubber stamps

While I use a lot of traditional rubber stamps for the projects in this book, I highly recommend the new clear polymer stamps. They are the ultimate stamping tool! Because placement can be critical to your projects, these clear stamps make alignment so easy a novice will look like a professional. I describe these "new wave" stamps more on page 13.

Inks

Using the proper ink for your project ensures its success. I often use Decor-it inks for many stamping projects. It is a quick drying ink that is permanent. I have also used Adirondack dye-based inks. These inks are not only wonderful for dying papers, but also for staining gourds. I also highly recommend Fabrico pigment inks. They are a "one size fits all" ink if you are just getting started. You can emboss with them, you can use them on shrink plastics, they are permanent when heat set, they give beautiful effects on metals. They are ideal for staining papier maché items and are wonderful for stencilng on walls because they will wash off if you don't like it. Last, but not least, they are water clean-up.

☞ Hint on Ink ☜

If you need quick drying ink for paper, then use dye-based inks. If you need quick drying ink that is also waterproof, Decor-it inks work great when applied with a make-up sponge. Remember Fabrico inks are only waterproof after they are heat set. So choose your inks according to the needs of the moment.

Heat tool

This tool is indispensable! Not only is it great for embossing safely, but you can use it to shrink plastic, heat foam and set inks on metal.

My favorite heat tool is Ranger's Heat-it. Some heat tools get too hot. This one is just right for my needs. It is quiet, easy to hold, has no exposed metal parts and doesn't blow embossing powder all over the place while you are trying to melt it. It also has a large heating area which makes heating foam and candles easier. If I could get it to do housework, my life would be complete!

Paper

In this book you will see how to transform ordinary laser paper and dye-based inks into beautiful hand-dyed papers. Also, in some of the gallery projects, paper wood veneers are used (shown on the bottom of the facing page). These veneers, which come in standard letter size, are easily cut with scissors. See page 119 for more information.

Embossing powders

Wow! What can I say about the powders available today? Now you can get beautiful matching inks and powders to coordinate your projects. If you are new to stamping, you will be amazed at how gorgeous impressions are when they are embossed with metallic powders.

⚘ How to Emboss ⚘

Embossing is quite easy to do. You simply stamp your design using a pigment ink (or a dye-based ink if you work fast), sprinkle embossing powder over it, tap off the excess and heat until it turns shiny and bonds to the paper.

Cutting tools

You will need a variety of tools to cut and punch many different types of objects. Useful cutting tools include a craft knife, hole punch, wire cutters and regular scissors.

Beads

Beads are an art form of their own, but when you combine them with various stamping projects they add interesting effects. The tiny glass beads open

up infinite possibilities! Try making your own beads with polymer clays.

Shrink plastic

Try making all kinds of projects with shrink plastic: buttons, pins, charms and jewelry. It comes in various colors and thicknesses. It is easiest to shrink with a heat tool, but it will shrink just as well in an oven.

Glues and adhesives

Special materials like Almost Leather and Metal Quilting need special glues to attach them to other surfaces. Spray adhesives (such as Super 77 from 3M) is excellent for these products as well as paper. It leaves no ripples in the paper and dries fairly fast. Double-sided foam tape also works well when you want to add a raised dimension to your projects. Jewel Bond works great for beads and other accessories.

Another great tape is Ultimate Bond. It comes in sheet form, as well as in varying widths. You can emboss on it and it will not melt. It is fabulous for holding on glass beads (see the glass bead purse project). It is also great for gold leaf and other foils.

Brayer

I love the brayer from Ranger Industries. It is made from a wonderful material that you can burn designs into with a wood burner to make your own rolling stamp. It has little feet on the sides that keep inks and paints off your work surface when you set it down.

Penscore

This great foam is wonderful for creating your own texture stamps. Reheat it and you can take the old design off and mold a new one!

Almost Leather

This is a unique foam product that looks and feels just like leather when you heat it with a heat tool and apply permanent inks.

Metal Quilting

This is 36-gauge real copper sheeting that is easy to tool with a stylus or pen.

Gold Leaf

This incredibly thin foil is wonderful for all kinds of uses. Clay, tape, frames and foam are just a few of the surfaces that it can be applied to.

DynaVinyl

This material and other static cling vinyls work great for the stained-glass look projects. They make great decals that you can embellish glassware with.

Clay

I love working with all the air dry and oven bake clays. Polymer clay, which must be oven baked in order to cure properly, comes in several different brands, and each has unique qualities. Find the one that's best for you. Air dry clay does not require an oven to cure, and is lighter than polymer clay, but less durable.

Dimensional Magic

This is a clear liquid which comes in many colors and is wonderful for adding a raised look to cards, wood, metal, plastic and more. It is water clean-up which makes it easy to use.

Hint: It takes a while to dry, but if you try to speed up the drying time with a heat tool, it can sometimes bubble, so use caution!

Accessories

You will want to have an array of beads, stones, threads, tassels and wires to embellish your finished projects. But don't stop there. Let your imagination go wild. Old keys, watch parts, thrift store finds and of course buttons and charms are also wonderful additions.

ꝗ Getting Centered ꝗ

So many people have told me over the years how stamping brought them out of depression, boredom and even lowered their blood pressure! I guess the joy of doing something you love and then sharing it with others really is the best medicine. If you have time to volunteer, consider showing the wonders of stamping to people in nursing homes, hospitals, etc. Anyone can do it and what it can do for self-esteem is amazing in a world where most things are done for us.

New Wave Stamps

Rubber stamping has been around for quite a while now. We have all experienced the problem of how to store and find the hundreds of stamps we have accumulated when we want to use them.

Unmounted stamps have grown in popularity over the past few years. Not only are they less expensive to purchase, but they are much easier to catalog and store compared to wood-mounted stamps. They take up a fraction of the space and are much easier to use when temporarily mounted on acrylic blocks. This eliminates the need for stamp positioners. You can clearly see where your stamp is placed.

Now there is a new generation photopolymer stamp that is an improvement over traditional rubber stamps. This high-grade polymer stamp is unaffected by permanent inks and solvent cleaners. You can see exactly where your design will be placed. It is perfect for lining up border stamps or joining two stamps together without a break in the line. The card to the left shows a great illustration of this. The tree and gate portion of the design is all on one stamp. The picket fence is a separate stamp. Because the stamps are clear, the alignment was a breeze! The small grass stamp is also a separate stamp.

These stamps are also easier to clean, as they can be placed under running water. Many companies are now offering unmounted stamps. Watch for this trend to continue.

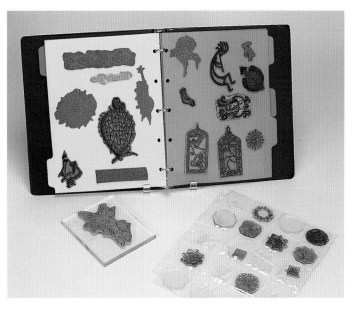

Creating an easy filing system for your stamps becomes a snap when you use unmounted stamps. Special sleeves for storing stamps can be purchased from office supply stores.

The images align perfectly when your stamps are mounted on acrylic blocks. Even though this card was made with several different images, everything aligns perfectly.

 Stamp credits: Print Blocks and Comotion

personal papers & stamps

Receiving a handmade card is a joy in an age of commercially produced sentiments.

Taking the time to handmake a card or gift conveys to the recipient that you feel they are special.

Although there are many types of papers available from all over the world, many people enjoy making their own paper from pulp and natural ingredients. You may think you don't have time to make your own paper, but in this section I will show you how to transform ordinary laser paper into personal expression. I will also show you the wonderful possibilities in using Penscore to make your own stamps. Making your own stamp is not hard—trust me! Just look around you and take impressions from ordinary objects, such as the bottom of your own shoe.

Make your own stamp

This versatile foam allows you to create your own texture stamp. If you get bored with one texture, simply reheat the foam and design a new one using any textured object you want!

supplies

- Penscore foam block
- anything with texture (basket, raffia, paper clip, shoe)
- Decor-it metallic inks (optional)
- ink pad
- paper
- heat tool

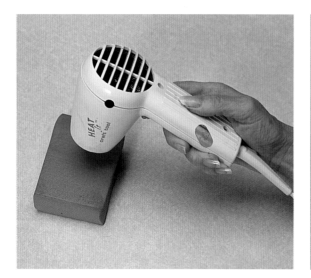

1 Heat the block until soft, about thirty seconds.

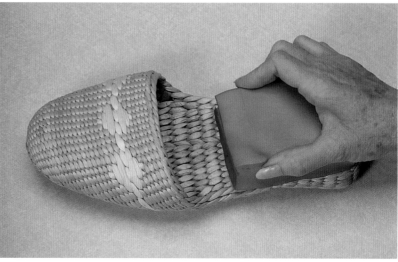

2 Quickly press it onto a textured surface.

3 The texture has now created a stamp!

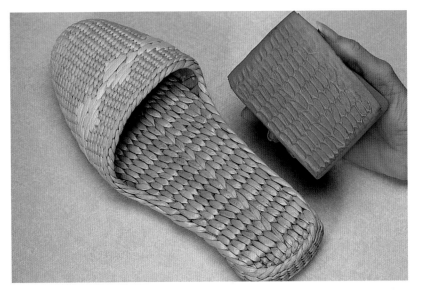

4 Ink the stamp and press it onto your stamping surface.

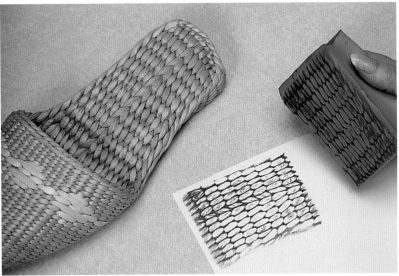

5 Clean the stamp and reheat the foam to remove the old design, and press it onto a new surface to make a new stamp! Penscore can be heated over and over to create new textures.

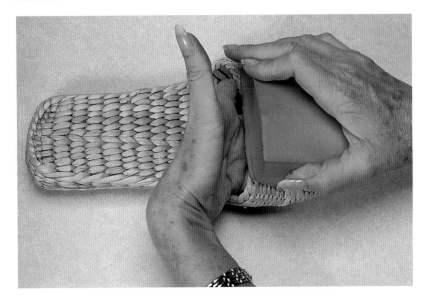

6 Experiment with different areas on the same object.

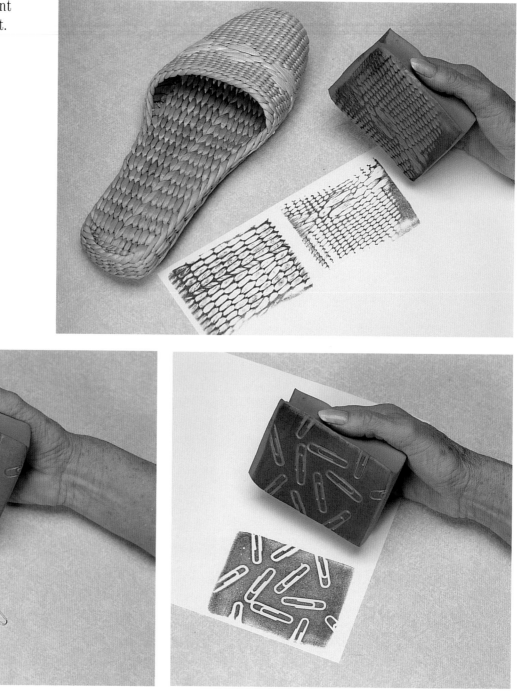

7 Randomly lay objects in a pile for an interesting effect.

8 The light and dark areas create a striking look.

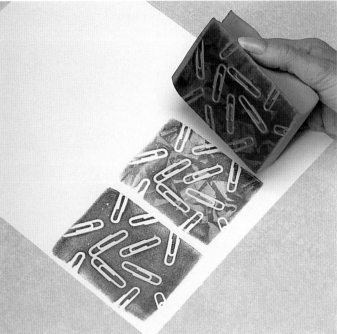

9 Ink the stamp, then remove some of the ink with crumpled paper for a batik look.

10 Get two different looks from the same stamp.

11 Raffia makes a great background, too.

12 Rainbow ink pads add interest as well.

13 Use the texture stamps to add metallic inks to hand-dyed papers for an elegant finishing touch.

Design your own paper

Beautiful papers are a very important aspect of stamping. Receiving a handmade card is a joy in an age of commercially produced sentiments. Taking the time to handmake cards or gifts conveys to the recipients that you feel they are special.

There are many types of papers available from all over the world. Many people enjoy making their own paper from pulp and natural ingredients.

This project demonstrates how you can transform ordinary laser printer paper and dye-based inks into inexpensive designer papers for backgrounds, wrapping paper and stamping surfaces.

supplies

* Butterscotch and Pitch Black Adirondack ink pads
* your choice of paper
* spray bottle of water
* paper towels
* heat tool

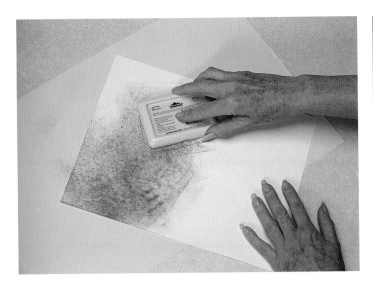

1 Carefully remove the lid from the first ink pad, (and rub it over the entire paper surface).

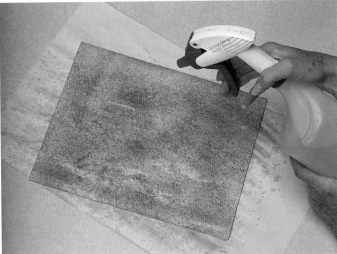

2 Spray the paper with water until the ink bleeds together.

3 Dab off the excess water with a paper towel.

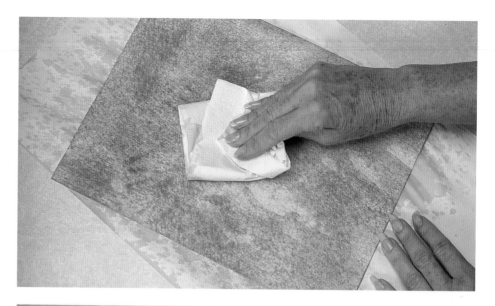

4 Dry the paper with a heat tool.

5 Crumple the paper to create texture. Carefully unfold the paper and lay it flat.

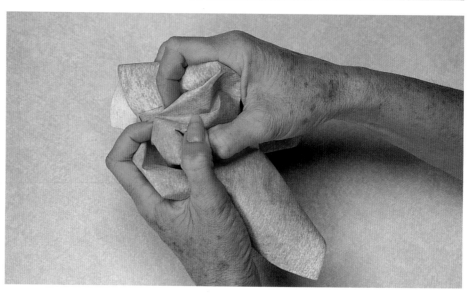

6 Remove the lid from the second ink pad, and rub it firmly over the textured areas.

7 Spray with water again.

8 Dab off the excess water and heat-dry, or air-dry if time permits.

✐ The finished paper.

✐ The finished paper wrapped around a box and tied with raffia and embellished with charms.

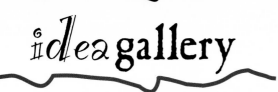

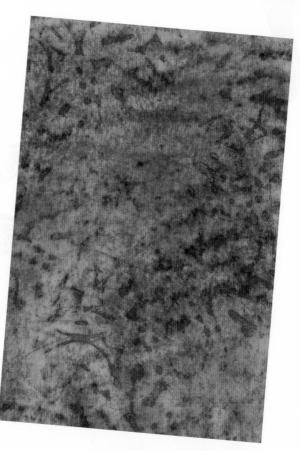

❧ This look was
achieved with
Penscore and inks.

❧ Make creases across the
paper instead of crumpling it
for a different effect.

❧ This paper was made in
the same way as the project
paper on the opposite page.

This background was inked and then textured with Penscore.

These bookmarks were sponged with dye-based inks and then sprayed with water to cause the colors to bleed. The Charles Rennie Mackintosh–inspired designs are by Michelle Ward for Comotion.

These die-cut boxes were sponged with Adirondack inks, then textured with Penscore stamps and more inks.

courage...
courage
allows
the words
of your
inner voice
to become
song.

Vesta—2000

❧ The edges of this center image were given a torn look by deep cutting with deckle scissors.

Stamp credits: ERA Graphics and Comotion

❧ This interesting stamp design from ERA Graphics was first stamped with black ink, then embossed with clear powder. Then inks were sponged onto the edges to harmonize with the background paper. Layering adds texture.

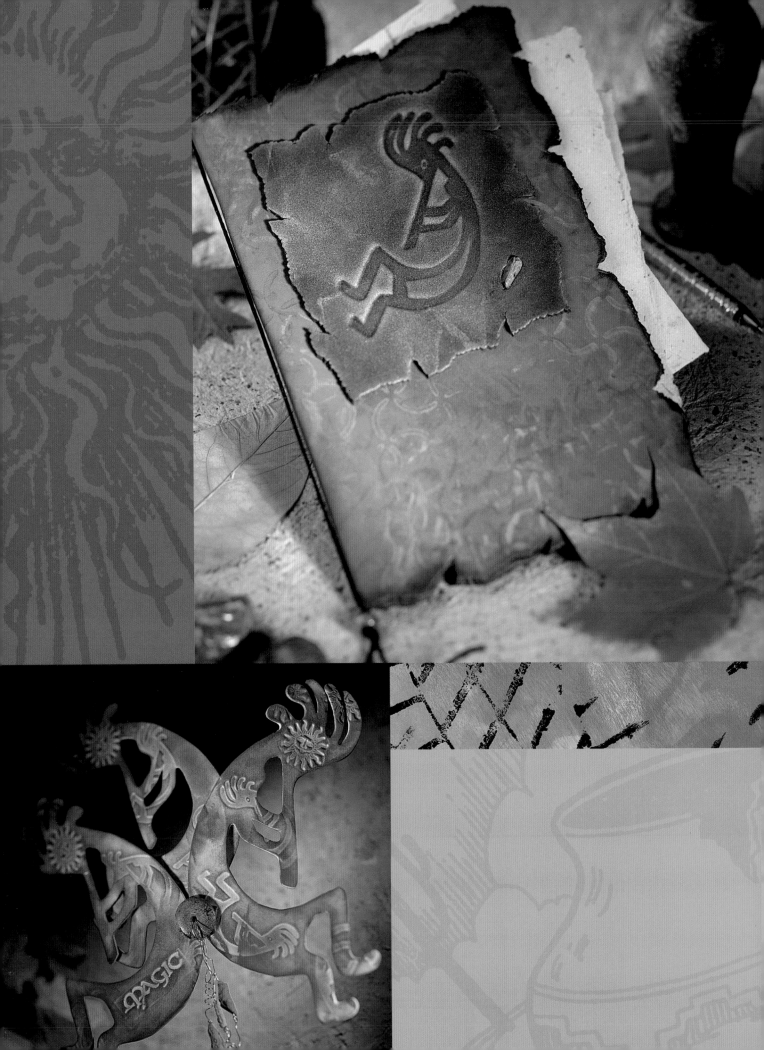

almost leather

Almost Leather was born one day while I was preparing samples for an upcoming trade show. I had some pieces of this interesting foam on my work table, and it just happened to get in the way of my heat tool.

The next thing I know I'm stamping on this softened foam, and wow! The impression stayed fixed after it cooled. When I sponged permanent inks on the background to make it look textured, it looked and felt so much like real leather I expected to get fan mail from cows.

Almost Leather has come a long way since then. Decor-it ink works great with this foam because the ink is waterproof and does not require heat setting. The white foam allows any color sponged on it to look vibrant. The black is stunning with colors as well as metallic shades. When mahogany ink is sponged on the tan and brown, the result is a real leather look.

This material is great for wall hangings and note cards because it is so lightweight. The uses are endless.

Wall Hanging

This project looks like it is made of terra cotta, but is lighter in weight and much more durable.

1 Stamp your main image with black ink on the top right corner of a sheet of copy machine paper.

2 Enlarge the design to the full size of the paper. Cut it out; you will use this as your template.

3 Lay the template on white Almost Leather, trace three times, then cut out.

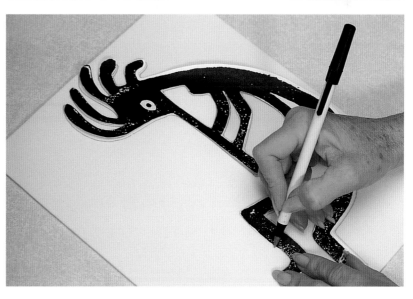

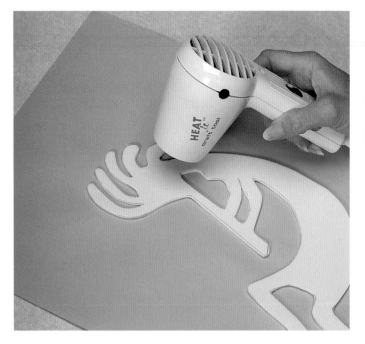

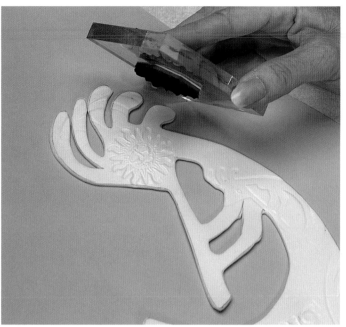

4 Heat both sides of the Almost Leather until it is smooth.

5 While the Almost Leather is still hot, stamp your images randomly, leaving a texture. Keep reheating areas to stamp until the designs cover the surface.

6 On scrap paper, squeeze out small amounts of your chosen inks.

7 With a makeup sponge, very lightly rub your brown ink all over the front and back of the image.

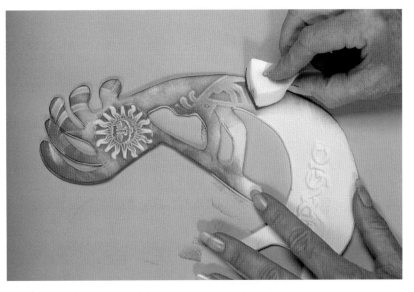

8 Randomly sponge on your other ink.

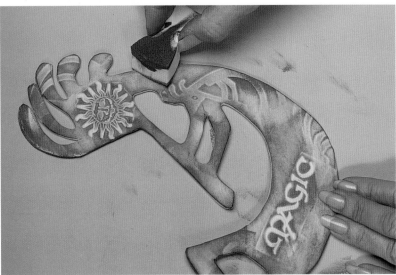

9 The materials I used to make the medallion are a ¼" dowel, one large clay bead, an assortment of small clay beads and gold or copper wire (cut three 18" pieces of wire). You can purchase clay beads at craft stores or bead shops or make your own from clay.

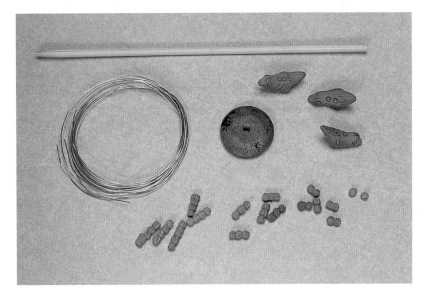

10 Fold the wires in half and feed them through the hole in the large bead. Run the ends back through the loop.

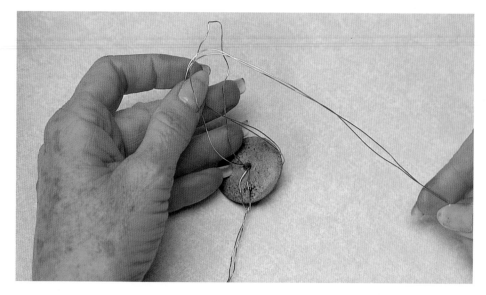

11 Pull the wires down tight.

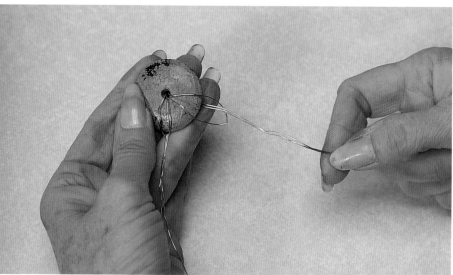

12 Tie a knot in each wire randomly and add a bead. Knot again to secure.

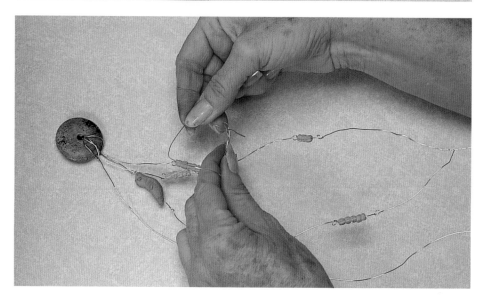

13 Leave long areas between each bead to coil around a dowel.

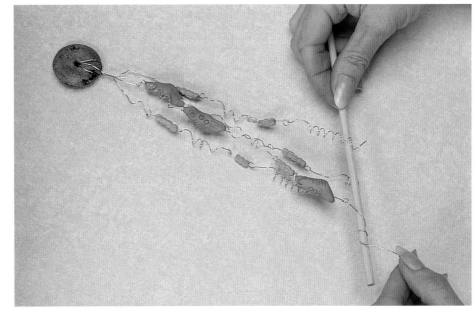

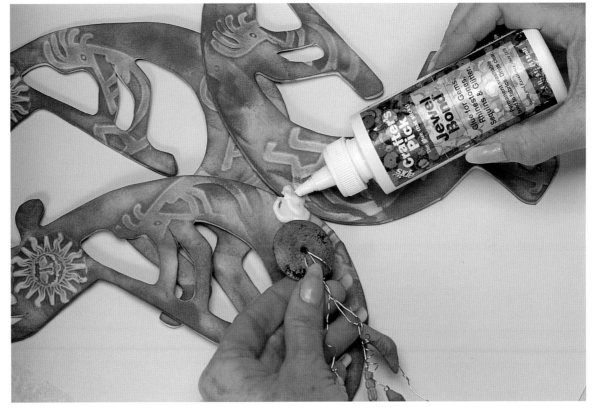

14 Arrange the pieces however you like and glue together the areas that touch. Glue the bead ornament to the center of the wall hanging.

Book Cover

If you like buying paperback books for friends and relatives, why not make a beautiful cover to go with it?

supplies

* brown Almost Leather sheet
* black Almost Leather sheet
* Kokopelli stamp (Out West)
* Penscore foam block
* anything with texture (basket, raffia, shoe)
* Mahogany, Verdigris and Gold Decor-it inks
* black permanent ink
* small stone
* 24" (61cm) black cord
* bead to secure cord
* heat tool
* deckle scissors
* craft knife
* makeup sponges
* spray adhesive
* scrap paper
* pen
* Jewel Bond glue

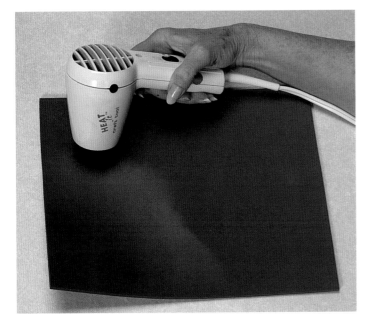

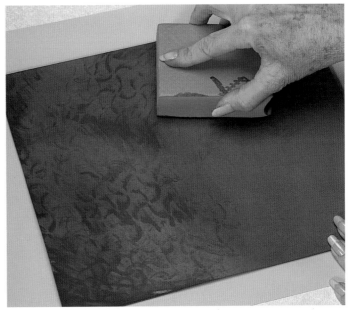

1 Using the heat tool, heat both sides of the brown Almost Leather completely until in shrinks evenly and looks smooth and leathery.

2 Create a texture stamp with foam. (See the Make Your Own Stamp project on page 16.) Squeeze your first selection of ink onto scrap paper. Ink the foam and randomly stamp on the leather piece to add texture.

3 Repeat with a second color of ink.

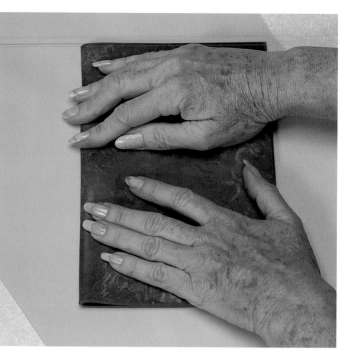

4 Fold the book cover in half, holding tightly while heating the edge with the heat tool.

5 Press the edge down while cooling; the book cover should stay closed now.

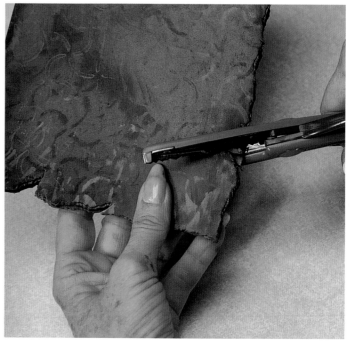

6 While holding firmly, slightly trim the edges with deckle scissors.

7 Notch the leather here and there to give it a torn look.

8 Squeeze out a small amount of black permanent ink onto scrap paper. Sponge onto the edges of the book cover to give an aged look.

9 Cut a piece of black Almost Leather (4½" x 4½" or 11.5cm x 11.5cm) using deckle scissors. Heat both sides until soft, then stamp.

10 Here I'm adding a turquoise stone on the lower right of the image and tracing around it with a pen.

11 Cut a hole with a craft knife so the stone will drop into it.

12 Lightly sponge on your second ink around the stamp area. Repeat with your third choice of ink.

13 Spray adhesive onto the back of the black piece and let it dry for ten minutes. Press it onto the upper portion of the book cover. Glue the stone in place.

14 Fold the cord in half and place it half inside, half outside the cover. Pull the ends together tightly and knot. Feed a bead onto the cords, pull up to knot and knot again.

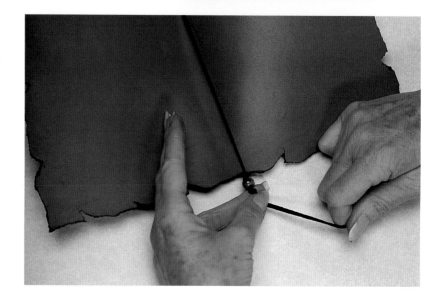

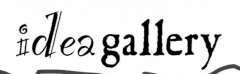
idea gallery

 A small book cover or photo album can be made with a half sheet of Almost Leather. Mahogany Decor-it ink was used to "stain" the brown foam.

Stamp credit: Arts Factory

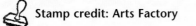 This small book cover was also made with a half sheet of Almost Leather. Violet and Gold Decor-it inks were sponged on the clay faces. The beads and feather were glued with Jewel Bond.

Stamp credit: Arts Factory

This fun hair barrette made from Almost Leather was sponged with Violet and Verdigris Decor-it inks. A plastic drink stir holds the hair in place.

 Stamp credit: Out West

Here's another playful barrette made by enlarging a stamp, such as this dragonfly design. I added texture by stamping on the foam (after heating), then embellished with a few beads.

 Stamp credit: ERA Graphics

Experiment with unusual rods for your barrettes. Here I used a special stick from Africa.

Stamp credit: Personal Stamp Exchange

◎∽ Similar in appearance to the hair barrette, this dragonfly serves as a great plant
pal. Write information on its back and feel
free to stick it out in the garden—Almost
Leather is completely waterproof.

 Stamp credit: ERA Graphics

◎∽ This card was embellished
with a top layer of Almost Leather.

Stamp credit: Print Blocks

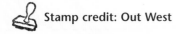 Even this address book had room for improvement.

Stamp credit: Out West

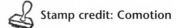 This film can was sponged with Decor-it inks. The top piece is Almost Leather sponged with the same colors.

Stamp credit: Comotion

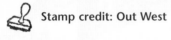

Almost Leather makes great journal covers.

Stamp credit: Out West

Here is a journal cover that includes glass beads. See the Beautiful Beads and Embossing Powders section for more about the technique.

metal works

Metal is a versatile medium that can be quilted, punched, embossed and more.

Metal that is 36 gauge or less is really easy to tool. Copper sheets or rolls are widely available, as well as other colors. Copper gives a really elegant look to stamping projects. Other surfaces such as wood, plastic, clay or foam, give the metal "body" to help it keep its shape.

Copper sheets, when heated or set directly on a hot plate or electric stove, will reveal a beautiful mix of colors. Unfortunately, this will not happen with colors that are on aluminum.

Metal antiquing gives the surface an old or weathered look. Heat-set inks are used when antiquing, but don't forget to experiment with paints, embossing powders, sand, and texturing tools.

Gold leaf is real gold pressed into an extremely thin sheet that can be rubbed onto many different surfaces to give a precious metal appearance. While gold leaf takes a little getting used to, it is well worth the effort. It adds dazzling effects to many crafting projects. Use it to cover wood, plastic, foam, paper and clay.

Metal Quilting Frame

This copper and tile frame is easier to make than it looks. Puffing the designs adds texture and heating the metal brings out a variety of natural colors.

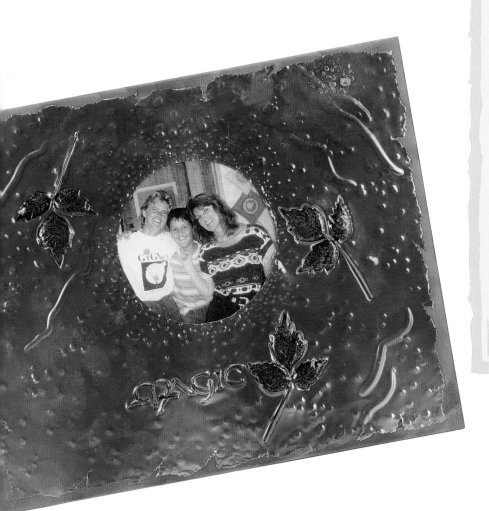

supplies

* copper Metal Quilting sheet
* Almost Leather (optional)
* 8" x 10" (20cm x 25cm) tile
* leaf stamp (Kodomo No Kao)
* magic stamp (Comotion)
* Mahogany Decor-it ink
* black permanent ink
* Dimensional Magic
* circle template
* photograph
* decorative easel (optional)
* ruler
* craft knife
* deckle scissors
* double-ball stylus
* wooden spindle
* spray adhesive
* heat tool or hot plate
* makeup sponge

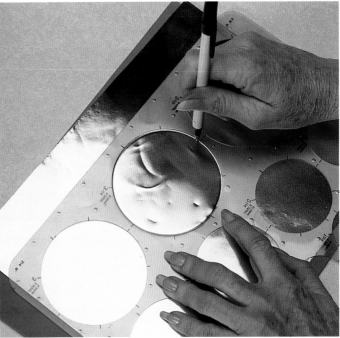

1 I like to lay the metal on top of the Almost Leather as a work surface. Mark the middle of the metal piece.

2 Place the circle template slightly higher than the mark. Trace with a pen or stylus.

3 Cut out the circle with a craft knife.

4 Using permanent ink, stamp your images.

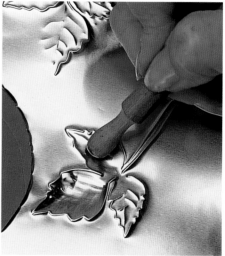

6 Turn the piece over and puff the designs with a wooden spindle.

5 Draw around the designs with a stylus to "quilt."

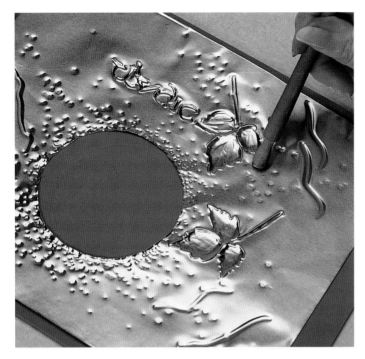

7 Draw the lines and pound with a spindle to create texture.

8 With deckle scissors, trim the edges of the metal to fit inside the tile piece.

9 Heat the metal until it turns different colors. Colors will change much faster with a hot plate or electric stove.

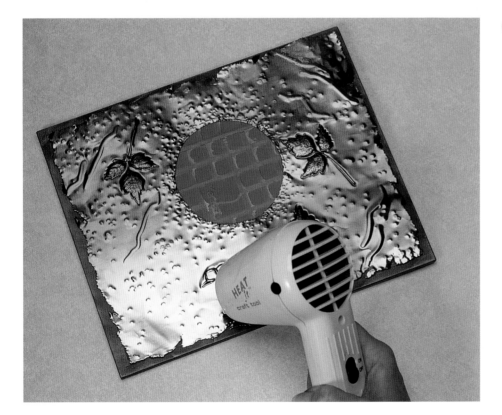

10 Fill the puffed images with Dimensional Magic to keep them from caving in. Let dry for several hours.

11 When Dimensional Magic is dry, spray the back of the piece completely with spray adhesive. Let dry for ten minutes and spray the same side again. Set aside.

12 With a makeup sponge, dab your selected in around the edges of the back of the tile piec

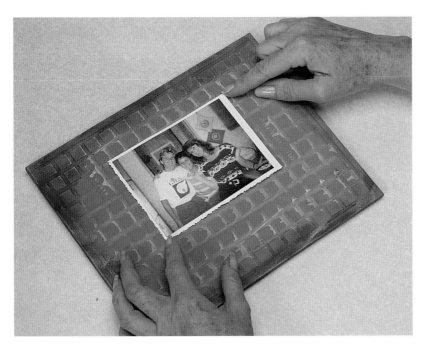

13 Tape the picture in place.

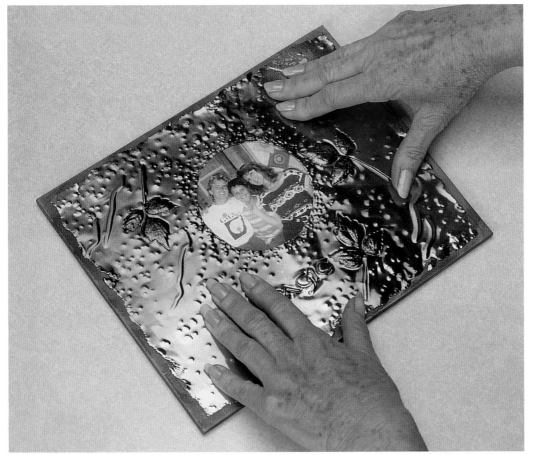

14 Lay the metal frame down over the picture. Press in place. Set on an easel to display.

Metal Antiquing

This is an easy way to make the copper sheeting look aged. Experiment with different textures using Penscore foam stamps and Fabrico inks.

supplies

* copper metal quilting sheet
* Almost Leather sheet
* hand stamp (ERA Graphics)
* Peony Purple and Burgundy Fabrico inks
* permanent black ink
* heat tool
* brayer
* double-ball stylus
* deckle edge scissors
* wooden spindle
* double-sided foam tape
* makeup sponges

1 Place the metal quilting sheet on Almost Leather as a work surface. Using permanent black ink, stamp your design onto the copper sheet.

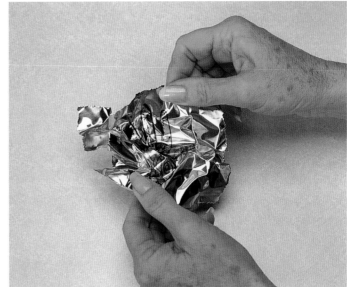

2 Cut around the design with deckle scissors to create a square. Carefully wrinkle up the metal piece.

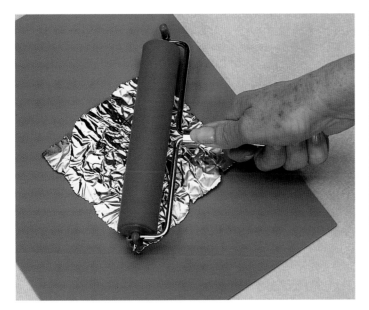

3 Lay the metal on top of the Almost Leather sheet. Smooth it out using a brayer.

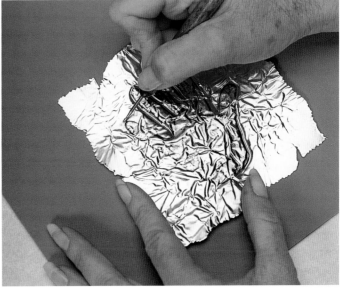

4 Draw around the design with a stylus to create a quilted look.

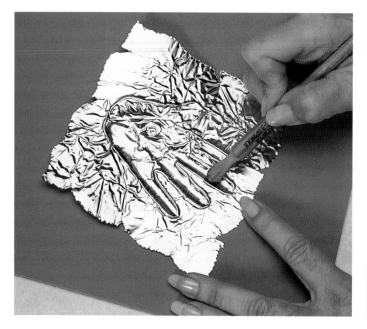

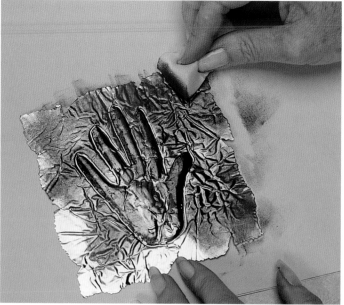

5 Turn the piece over and lay it back down on the Almost Leather sheet. Rub the inside design with the wooden spindle to puff the image.

6 Using makeup sponges, dab on one ink randomly. Set it with a heat tool.

7 Dab on a second color of ink and heat it again.

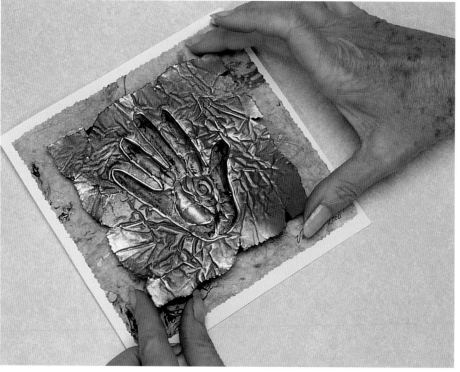

8 Cut pieces of double-sided foam tape and apply it to the back of the metal.

Rusted Lamp

I had great fun discovering Chemtek while I was in the photography studio at North Light Books. Chemtek is a superior metallic finish for new and aged appearances. It is environmentally friendly and gives an instant natural finish. Thanks for sharing this product Christine! (See the Resources section on page 126 for more information on Chemtek.)

supplies

- ☀ copper metal sheeting
- ☀ four-sided lamp (or any object that needs a new, exciting look)
- ☀ hand stamp (ERA Graphics)
- ☀ Steel and Rust Chemtek
- ☀ permanent black ink
- ☀ pergamano tool
- ☀ spray adhesive
- ☀ sandpaper
- ☀ brush

1 With a brush, basecoat the lamp with Steel Chemtek.

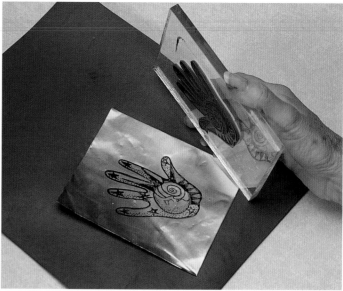

2 Cut out four equal-sized squares of copper metal sheeting. Stamp images on them with permanent black ink.

3 Sponge on another color of Chemtek.

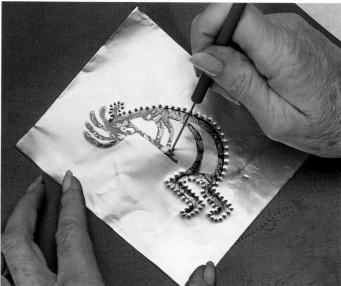

4 With a pergamano tool, poke holes around the image so that when the lamp is turned on, light will shine through.

5 Coat the finished metal pieces with spray adhesive.

6 Secure them to the now-rusted lamp.

7 Sand the rough edges.

Gold Leaf Frame

This is a fun material to use when you want to make wood look like metal. The gold leafing is heated to create interesting colors and texture. You will love how easily it adheres to any surface. Try covering plastic objects as well.

supplies

- flat wooden frame
- lizard and spiral stamps (Comotion)
- black ink pad
- gold paint (optional)
- Dimensional Magic, any color
- gold leaf sheets
- spray adhesive
- soft cloth
- heat tool

1 Stamp your images onto the frame using black ink. Heat-set the ink for two minutes. Squeeze Dimensional Magic onto the designs to give a raised texture.

2 Let dry for a few hours.

3 Spray the front and sides of the frame with spray adhesive. Let dry about ten minutes.

4 Carefully lay sheets of gold leaf onto the frame. Cover all areas using two different colors or patterns of gold leaf. Rub the entire frame with a soft cloth. Make sure you hold the frame over a shallow box or something that can catch extra bits of gold leaf.

5 Using the black ink pad, rub over raised stamp areas to create contrast.

6 Heat-set inked areas. Paint the back of the frame with gold paint if desired, or cover with more gold leaf.

idea gallery

 This interesting stamp design was high-lighted with a pergamano tool, then antiqued and embellished with wire and a bead.

Stamp credit: Arts Factory

 These designs lend themselves well to the "torn" aluminum. Harmonizing the ink colors with the stationery hues is key.

Stamp credit: Krafty Lady

This box is a fun use of the metal antiquing technique. Kokopellis were stamped with permanent ink, covered with Dimensional Magic, then inked with Fabrico inks to "antique."

Stamp credit: Comotion

 This copper Metal Quilting frame was heated to get variegated colors.

Stamp credits: Stamp Oasis (horse), Comotion (small spiral) and Rubber Stampede (large spiral)

 Here is a ready-made acrylic frame topped with Metal Quilting. Another picture is on the back.

Stamp credit: Comotion

 This cardboard box was sponged with Decor-it inks, then topped with puffed metal.

Stamp credit: Print Blocks

 Small leftover pieces of copper create interesting elements for cards and other small projects.

 Stamp credit: ERA Graphics

 This card was embellished with interesting paper layers and grass mat ribbon. It was topped with a piece of Almost Leather that was covered with gold leaf. A heat tool was used to soften the foam, and the hand design was stamped on with permanent black ink. A small bead was added as a final touch.

Stamp credit: ERA Graphics and Comotion

 This journal cover, made from Almost Leather, is embellished with a piece of Metal Quilting.

 Stamp credit: Comotion

✍ Here's another journal cover (made from papers by Paper Stuff) that shows how Almost Leather appears when gold leaf is applied.

Stamp credit: Out West

mixed media

This section shows what you can do with just about any item you find

lying around. Certainly this isn't the end all of mixed media; I wish

for this to be an inspiration for you to find different objects around

you and turn them into beautiful works of art.

Look around you at craft stores, thrift shops and flea markets.

That old, out of date thing in the sale barrel could probably be improved with just a little bit of imagination and a few stamping supplies!

Clay Stamping

Clay and stamping seem to go hand in hand. Whether creating molds or stamping directly in clay, the look is gorgeous and easy to do even for beginners.

There are many different clays on the market, from air-dry to oven-bake. Experiment and create your own look by adding elements such as gold leaf, sand, wood chips and glitter.

supplies

* Almost Leather sheet
* sun and moon face stamp (ERA Graphics)
* black polymer clay
* Decor-it metallic ink
* makeup sponge
* heat tool
* scrap paper
* brayer

1 Heat the center area of the Almost Leather until it is soft (a couple of minutes).

2 Quickly and firmly stamp the design on softened foam.

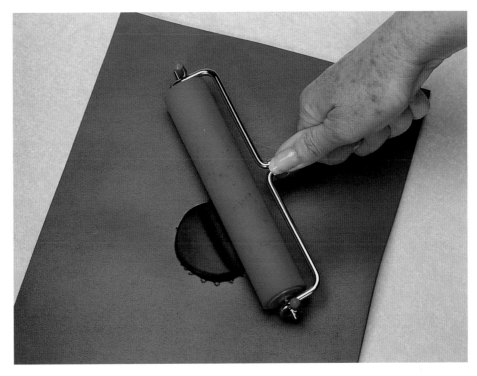

3 Roll a small ball of black polymer clay until it is soft and smooth. Flatten and place over the "mold." Roll a brayer over the clay to force it down into the design.

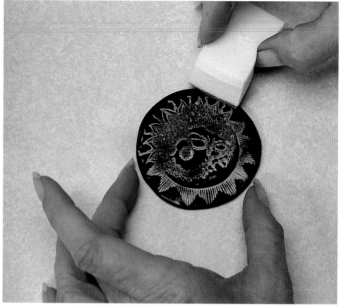

4 Carefully peel up the design and bake according to the manufacturer's directions.

5 When the clay has cooled, squeeze a small amount of metallic ink on scrap paper. Using a makeup sponge, very lightly rub ink across the design to bring out the image.

6 Use the clay as a card embellishment or jewelry.

idea gallery

❧ Black polymer clay and Gold and Verdigris Decor-it ink bring out the beautiful fish design by calligrapher Arthur Baker. The clay was embellished with charms for a finishing touch.

❧ Here is another Arthur Baker design. It adds simple elegance to this polymer clay pendant.

Shrink Plastic Box

There are many different kinds of shrink plastic—clear, frosted, white, black and others.

The first time I combined stamping with shrink plastic, I went crazy, staying up all night, trying "just one more stamp" to see how it looked after it had gyrated into a smaller version of its original size.

1 Use the heart box lid as a template to draw a heart on the shrink plastic.

2 Cut out the shrink plastic heart with scissors.

3 Lay the heart on the Almost Leather sheet (it makes a great stamping cushion). Stamp a design using permanent black ink.

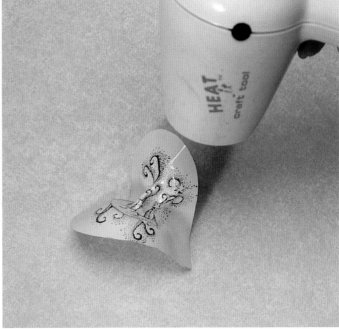

4 Shrink the heart with a heat tool.

5 The piece is done when it lies flat.

6 Using a makeup sponge, stain the box with your favorite ink.

7 If desired, add more ink with Penscore to give a textured look. (To learn how to use Penscore to add texture to your pieces, see page 37.)

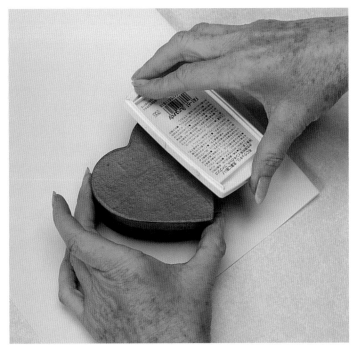

8 Using a pigment ink pad, dab ink all over the box lid.

9 Cover the entire lid with embossing powder.

10 Melt the powder with a heat tool, and while still hot, add another layer of powder.

11 While the embossing powder is still hot, drop a shrink-plastic heart on the lid. Keep heating, and drop stones here and there. Set aside to cool.

idea gallery

⟪ This bracelet is made with ultra thin shrink plastic (half the thickness of the regular kind). The angel design was punched before shrinking. Fabrico ink was sponged on afterward and then heat-set. The charms were added for fun.

⟪ The shrink-plastic centerpiece adds interest to this film can box.

 Stamp credit: Comotion

🌀 This necklace and earrings made of shrink plastic were given an enameled look with Adirondack embossing powders and tiny glass beads.

🌀 This necklace variation has movable parts joined together. Other elements were added to the shrink plastic to complete the look.

Dyna Vinyl

Stained glass is beautiful, and this faux method is fast and gives you the versatility to change the look of your glassware on a whim to meet any occasion. It is wonderful for a kid's birthday party, as all the guests can have fun making their own party favors to take home.

Your finished decals can be applied inside or outside the glassware. They are waterproof and can be washed.

supplies

* DynaVinyl sheet
* dragonfly stamp (ERA Graphics)
* black permanent ink
* iron-on fabric transfer ink
* Crystal Clear Gallery Glass Window Color
* Almost Leather (optional)
* scissors
* cotton swabs
* heat tool

1 Place the DynaVinyl sheet on top of the Almost Leather sheet to help leave a better stamp impression. Using permanent black ink, quickly stamp the designs before the ink dries.

2 Tint the stamp images with iron-on inks using cotton swabs. Set with a heat tool.

3 Squeeze on clear window color in a bumpy fashion to give a real stained glass look to the design. Let dry.

4 When dry, cut out the design. Peel the design off the paper backing. Place on glassware, window or anything else you can think of!

idea gallery

◎◇ Designs stamped on static cling vinyl and colored with glass stains add color and texture to glass.

Stamp credit: Comotion

◎◇ This stylish glass bowl becomes an instant fish bowl with these fun goldfish designs.

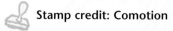

Stamp credit: Comotion

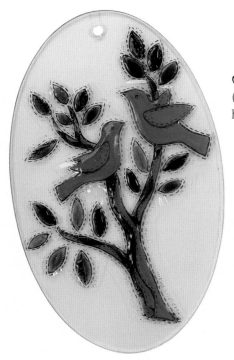

❧ Renee Remo's Mola design (Comotion) fits perfectly on this hanging glass ornament.

❧ This glass vase from Mexico looks like it was born with a Kokopelli on it!

 Stamp credit: Comotion

Gourd Art

Gourds are a fantastic surface for stamping. They have been used for centuries to create functional vessels. Not only are they simple to cut and sand, they are a breeze to stain with dye-based inks.

supplies

- ☀ gourd
- ☀ various stamps
- ☀ several dye-based ink colors
- ☀ black permanent ink
- ☀ threads and beads
- ☀ makeup sponges
- ☀ handsaw
- ☀ woodburning tool (optional)
- ☀ clear acrylic spray coating
- ☀ sandpaper

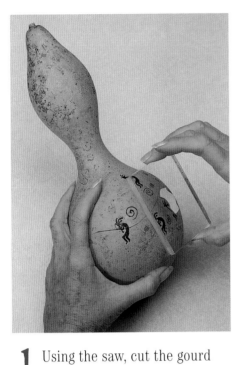

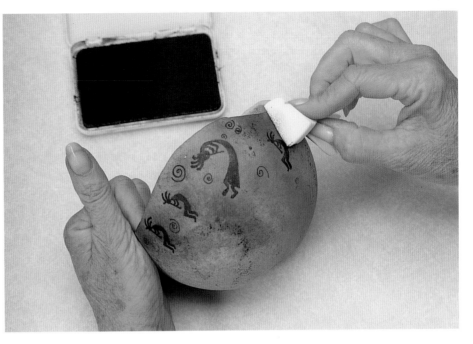

1 Using the saw, cut the gourd apart, creating a lid. Sand the edges smooth. Hold both pieces together and stamp designs with permanent ink.

2 Stain the gourd by applying various inks with makeup sponges. Spray the gourd with clear acrylic spray to seal the color.

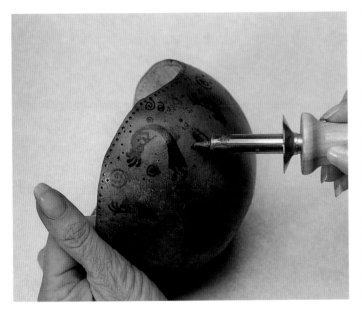

3 Use a woodburning tool to add interest if you like.

4 Tie beads with yarn for a finishing touch.

Candle Stamping and Embossing

Pardon the pun, but candles have become a really hot category in the crafting world. They are one of the items that soothe our stressed out environments, and it just seemed natural to find ways to stamp on them.

There are many types of ready-made candles, as well as kits to make your own. Don't forget to check out the discount stores to look for boring candles you can transform into beautiful works of art.

supplies

* dark-colored candle
* white or pastel candle
* various stamps
* Copper Decor-it ink
* black permanent ink
* bright rainbow ink pad
* white Unryu paper
* embellishments such as yarn and beads (optional)
* paper towels
* cotton swabs
* scissors
* makeup sponges
* heat tool
* scrap paper

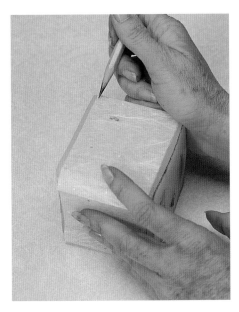

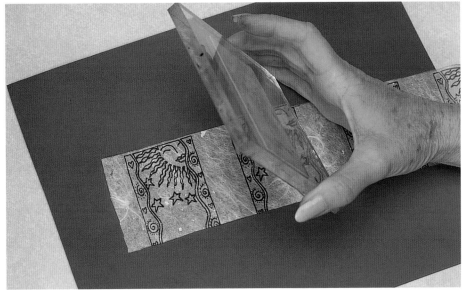

1 Cut the paper to fit around the white candle. It is best to cut the paper ¼" shorter than the candle's height.

2 Stamp designs using black permanent ink.

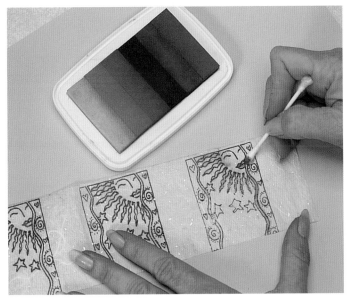

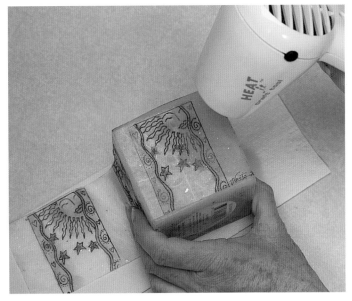

3 Using cotton swabs, color the designs with a rainbow ink pad.

4 Lay the stamped paper on top of the candle and hold it tight while heating wax with the heat tool. The paper will melt onto the candle. Continue to heat and press paper into the wax all the way around the candle.

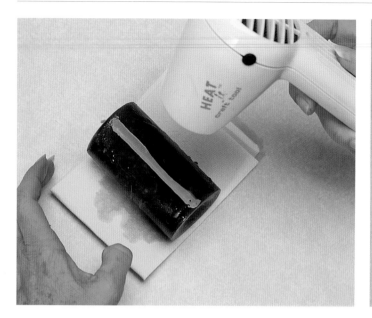

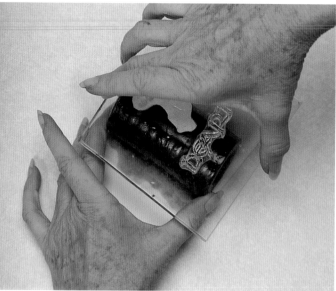

1 Lay the dark-colored candle on a folded paper towel to keep it from rocking. Heat the candle surface area to be stamped until it appears wet.

2 Let the candle cool slightly until the candle clouds over. Quickly stamp onto the melted wax.

3 Hold the stamp in the wax for a few seconds, then carefully rock the stamp until it releases easily from the candle.

4 Squeeze a little ink of your choice on scrap paper. Using a makeup sponge, lightly rub ink across the stamped areas of the candle to create contrast. Add yarns and beads to embellish.

idea gallery

 The same stamp designs used in the step-by-step project were applied to this square candle. Notice that light-colored candles don't produce as much contrast as dark ones do.

Stamp credits: Out West and Comotion

 When stamping onto papers and melting them onto candles, it is best if both the papers and the candles are light colored. This paper has beautiful gold strings in it.

Stamp credit: Comotion

 This star candle was hand poured from a candle-making kit. The design was stamped on paper, cut out, then melted onto the candle. The glitter glue streaks were added randomly.

 Stamp credit: Comotion

 This pillar candle is embellished with a charm.

Stamp credit: Stamp Oasis

 A dragonfly charm was pressed into melted wax, then secured with a bead-top straight pin.

Stamp credit: ERA Graphics

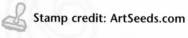 Metal Quilting adds interest to this candle.

Stamp credit: ArtSeeds.com

A rock-shaped candle is an interesting variation.

 **Stamp credit: Comotion**

beautiful beads & embossing powders

Tiny glass beads and embossing powders are a stunning combination.

The rough and smooth textures create an interesting contrast. Both stick easily to Ultimate Bond tape.

Embossing powders come in many different grains, formulations and colors. When heated with a heat tool, they melt and adhere to whatever surface they are applied to. While they add great texture and dimension to stamping, they are also a versatile art medium to use as a coating on many surfaces.

This section shows examples of boxes, journal covers, amulet bags and bookmarks that all use these two items plus a few others.

Embossing Powder Box

This is another opportunity to combine embossing powder, Metal Quilting and glass beads for a stunning effect!

supplies

- ☀ small heart-shaped papier maché box
- ☀ Eggplant Adirondack ink pad
- ☀ Gold or Copper Decor-it ink
- ☀ Cranberry and Eggplant Adirondack embossing powders
- ☀ clear embossing powder
- ☀ Ultimate Bond tape
- ☀ gold leaf crumbs
- ☀ two colors of glass beads
- ☀ spray acrylic topcoat
- ☀ heat tool
- ☀ scissors
- ☀ several colorful stones
- ☀ makeup sponges
- ☀ scrap paper
- ☀ pencil

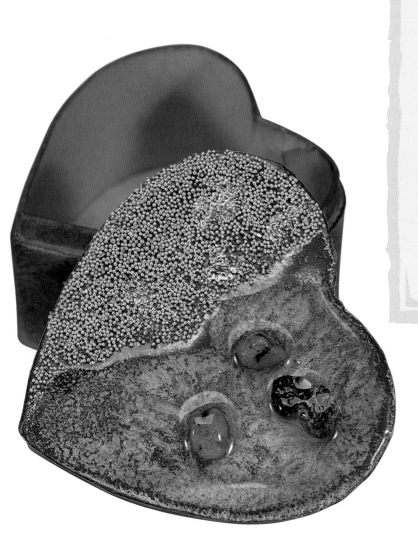

1 Remove the lid from the ink pad. Rub it directly all over the heart box and lid.

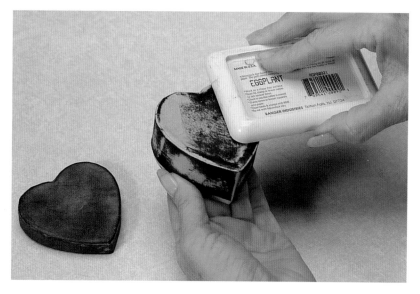

2 Blend and add more ink with a makeup sponge.

3 Lightly sponge on gold or copper ink to give a burnished look.

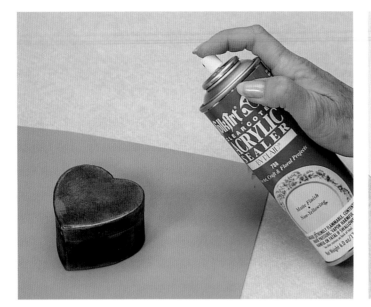

4 Spray the entire box with acrylic coating.

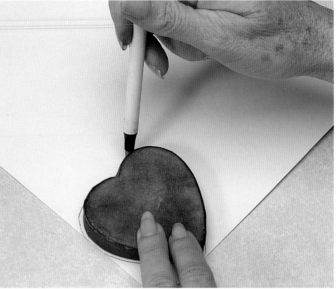

5 Place the heart box lid on a sheet of tape and trace.

6 Cut out the tape heart and remove one side of the paper backing.

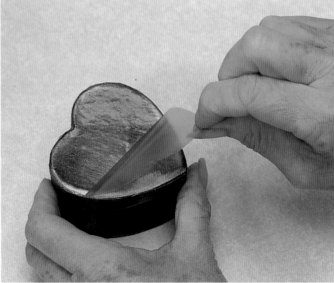

7 Place the sticky heart tape on the box lid, rub to adhere and remove the top paper.

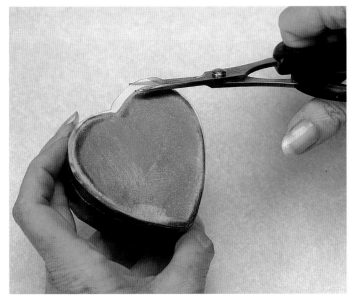

8 Trim any excess tape.

9 Place the box lid on scrap paper and pour some of the first color of embossing powder on the right side of the sticky tape, shaking off the excess and returning it to its bottle.

10 Pour your second color of embossing powder over the first to give it a marbled look.

11 Heat until melted.

12 While the embossing powders are still hot, pour on clear embossing powder.

13 Heat until melted.

14 Drop colored stones into the melted powder and let cool.

15 Wet your fingertip and pick up small amounts of gold leaf crumbs and place them randomly on the left side of the box.

16 Hold the lid over a dish and pour some of the glass beads onto the sticky tape. Return excess beads to their bottle.

17 Pour a different color of glass beads over the remaining uncovered tape. Rub beads firmly to set.

Glass Bead Purse

This is a great way to have fun with your stamping supplies (no stamps required!). Everyone will ask how long it took you to bead this charming little purse. Explore the many possibilities that this project creates through the use of gold leaf, Ultimate Bond tape and tiny glass beads!

supplies

- one sheet of Ultimate Bond tape (4½″ x 1½″ or 11.5cm x 3.8cm)
- ⅛″ (3.2mm) wide Ultimate Bond tape
- gold leaf sheet
- glass beads
- charms or beads
- scissors
- ¹⁄₁₆″ (1.5mm) hole punch
- jump rings
- needle-nose pliers
- cord, chain or necklace

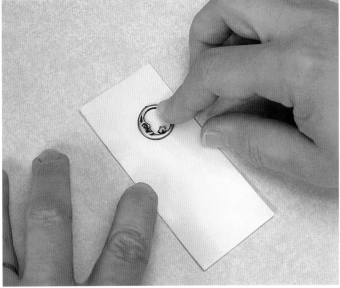

1 Cut a piece of Ultimate Bond tape about the size you would like your purse to be (mine is 4½" x 1½"). Remember that you will be folding this piece in half to form the purse. Peel one side of the backing off.

2 Choose charms and embellishments and press them onto the tape.

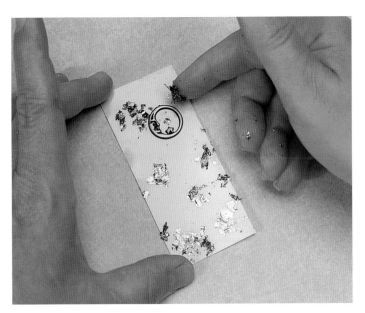

3 Randomly press some gold leaf onto the tape.

4 Sprinkle glass beads onto the tape. Do this over a dish or container so you can catch the excess.

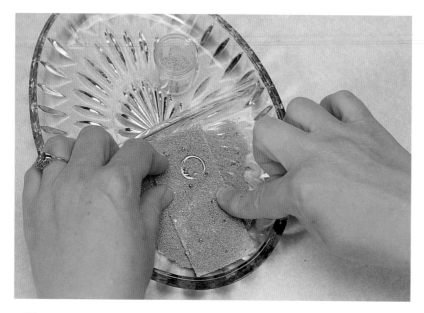

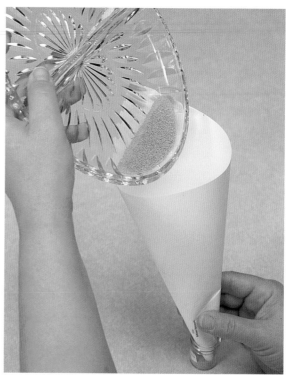

5 Repeat with another color of glass beads if you wish. Firmly press on the beads to make sure they adhere.

6 Funnel beads back into their bottle.

7 Remove the other side of the double-stick tape.

8 Place the sticky side on a sheet of gold leaf.

9 Remove the excess gold leaf from the edges until they are smooth.

10 Cut a small strip of ⅛" wide Ultimate Bond tape, and adhere it on what will become the top flap of the purse. Peel off the second backing.

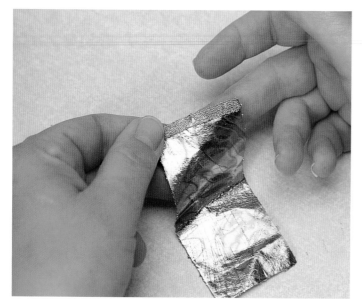

11 Fold down the top edge to form the top flap.

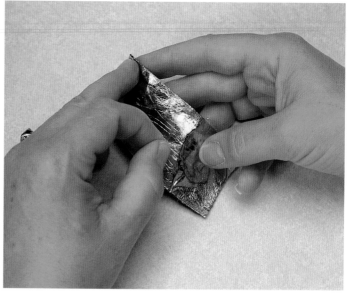

12 Cut another two strips of tape for the two sides of the purse. They should not extend to the top of the purse but allow space for the top flap to fold over.

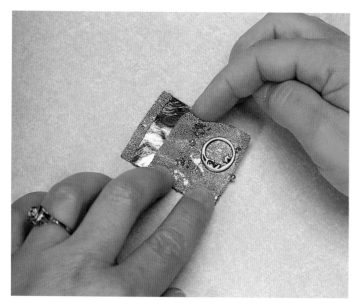

13 Peel the second backing off the tape, and fold your beaded strip onto itself to glue down the sides. This creates the pouch.

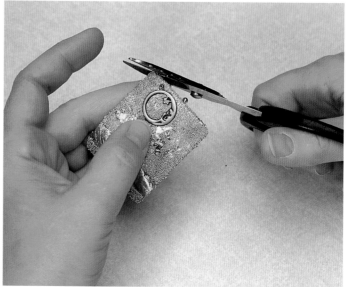

14 Gently round the bottom corners and top flap corners with scissors.

15 If you want to attach a cord, use a ¹⁄₁₆" hole punch to create holes for two jump rings.

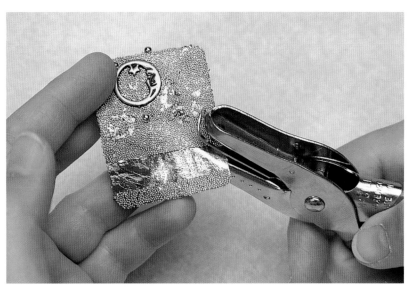

16 Punch additional holes anywhere you would like to attach charms.

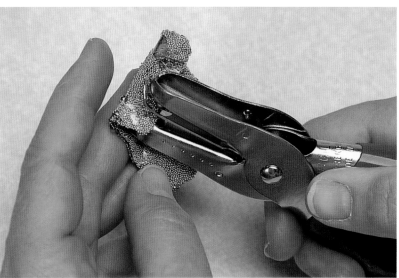

17 Attach jump rings and charms with needle nose pliers.

Light Switch Plate

No excuse for ordinary light switch plates after you learn this technique! A little ink and Dimensional Magic and you've got a three-dimensional wonder that will spruce up any home decor.

supplies

- light switch plate
- dragonfly stamp (Stamp Oasis)
- Mahogany, Verdigris and Copper Decor-it inks
- Dimensional Magic
- heat tool

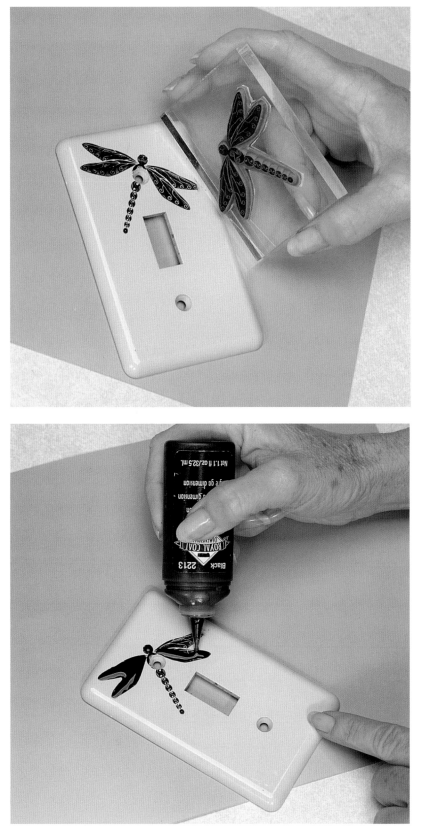

1 Stamp your image onto the plate.

2 Apply Dimensional Magic.

3 Cover the switch plate with your first chosen color of permanent ink.

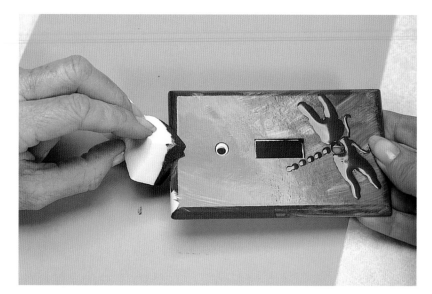

4 Add a complementing color of ink.

5 Add further highlights if you like.

❧ Tiny glass bottle pendants were a perfect surface to give a ceramic glaze look to Adirondack embossing powders and beads. A cotton swab was inserted into the top to hold the bottle while heating the powder.

❧ The top of this box was stained with Red Pepper Adirondack ink then embossed with clear Ultra Thick Embossing Enamel. A mixture of other powder colors was melted onto a release paper. When cool, the melted powders cracked off the release paper. The cracked pieces were laid on the box top after melting the clear powder again. The small pieces melted and now appear like mosaic designs.

✐ Here are some more mosaic looks, this time on black. The beads add texture.

AS I LET GO OF THE OLD WAY, A NEW WAY IS SHOWN TO ME.

✐ Ultra Thick Embossing Enamel Gold and Interference Blue were embossed on cardboard shapes. Pieces of copper Metal Quilting were dropped into the mixture before cooling. The paper is from Paper Stuff.

 Stamp credit: ERA Graphics

ᏬᎧ This film can was sponged with Violet and Platinum Decor-it inks. Ultra Thick Embossing Enamels were then applied to the top and stamped.

 Stamp credit: Comotion

ᏬᎧ Matching Adirondack inks and powders were used to create this box lid. Glass beads and gold leaf add texture. A charm was added while the powder was hot.

❧ Metal Quilting was added to these box lids for a dramatic effect.

 Stamp credit: ArtSeeds.com

❧ Here's a card embellished with shrink art.

Stamp credit: ERA Graphics

 Here are more embossed
images on cards.

Stamp credit: Comotion

These cards were embossed with powders that have glitter in them.

Stamp credit: Comotion

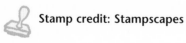

Here's an amulet bag with a shrink plastic surprise inside, made in the same way as the glass bead purse project.

Stamp credit: ERA Graphics

This large heart box was hand-dyed with Butterscotch Adirondack ink, then embossed with Butterscotch Adirondack embossing powder. It was further embellished with metal quilting, tiny gold and silver glass beads and gold leaf.

Stamp credit: Stampscapes

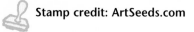 This small heart box was dyed with Cranberry Adirondack ink, then embossed with the matching embossing powder. Metal Quilting and glass beads were then added.

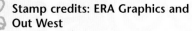 **Stamp credit: ArtSeeds.com**

 The center paper on this card was stamped and embossed on torn watercolor paper, tinted with Adirondack inks, then placed on Ultimate Bond tape and finished with gold leaf and glass beads.

Stamp credits: ERA Graphics and Out West

These three journal covers have Paper Stuff backgrounds. The top pieces are a mixture of embossing powders, gold leaf, glass beads and metal quilting.

Stamp credit (bottom right journal): ERA Graphics and Comotion

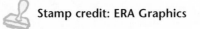 Here's another book cover with papers by Paper Stuff.

Stamp credit: ERA Graphics

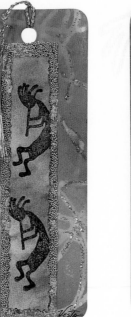

 These bookmarks are embellished with glass beads and embossing powders.

Stamp credits: Out West and ERA Graphics

Paper Wood

Just when you think you have stamped it all, along comes paper wood. Veneers have been around for a long time, but never has it been so easy to use. Easy to cut with regular scissors, this 8½" x 11" size (A4 equivalent) is just right for many projects.

There is nothing quite like the look and feel of real wood—bird's-eye maple, cedar, oak, walnut and aspen are but a few to choose from. Using several different woods on one project creates a wonderful contrast.

 This book cover was made of black Almost Leather and topped with pieces of bird's-eye maple and walnut to give it body.

Stamp credits: Stampscapes and Comotion

✐ This luminaria was made with a single sheet of veneer and one sheet of copper, each cut into four pieces. Holes were punched through both layers so the light could shine through when placed over a candle.

Stamp credit: Stamp Oasis

Cherish your visions and your dreams as they are the children of your soul

✐ A fun picture frame was created from veneer glued onto Almost Leather.

Stamp credits: Comotion and ArtSeeds.com

❧ Chevrons were created out of veneer scraps and then glued to this heart box lid. Clear embossing ink was applied to the lid and then embossed with several layers of clear Ultra Thick Embossing Enamel. A few sprinkles of gold embossing powder adds interesting effects.

❧ A bit of gold leaf topped with clear Dimensional Magic divides these two veneers.

Glitter Glue

Adding a hint of glitter glue to cards gives a finishing touch like nothing else can. It takes a little getting used to, however. You don't want to squeeze too hard or you can get more than you wanted on your creations. If this happens, quickly remove some of it with a cotton swab. Most of the time no harm is done if you catch it before it begins to dry.

Glitter glues come in a variety of colors, which look beautiful on dark papers. Crystal can also be used to add sparkle without affecting the color underneath it.

If you are stamping on fabrics and want the glitter glue effect, be sure it is permanent; regular glitter glue will wash out.

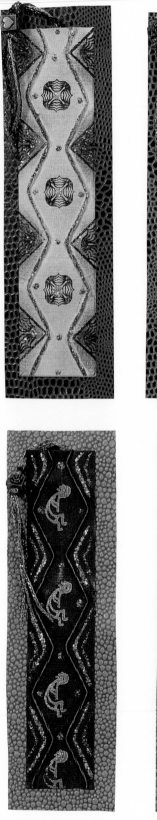

❧ This channeled paper works great for tiny stamps. Glitter glue beads add sparkle as well as texture.

 Stamp credits: Out West and ArtSeeds.com

 These bookmarks were dyed with dye-based inks and sprayed with water, stamped with permanent black ink. then embellished with glitter glue.

Stamp credits: ArtSeeds.com, Viva Las Vegastamps, Kodomo No Kao, Stamp Oasis, Stampscapes and ERA Graphics

These designs are interesting with this mix of paper textures.

Stamp credit: Comotion

A prickly pear stamp was sponged with inks and glitter glue. The stones and bead were glued to the corrugated cardboard strip.

Stamp credit: Out West

 Channeled paper creates an interesting background for these designs. Glitter glue is used sparingly.

Stamp credit: ERA Graphics

 Glitter glue was gently squeezed onto these fish stamps.

Stamp credit: ERA Graphics

Resources

Rubber Stamps

Arthur Baker
contact through ArtSeeds.com

ArtSeeds.com
P.O. Box 37041
Tucson, AZ 85740
(520) 219-0407
www.artseeds.com

Uptown Design Co.
(Comotion products)
10 Caledonia Summit
Browns Point, WA 98422
(800) 888-3212
(253) 925-1234
www.uptowndesign.com

ERA Graphics
2476 Ottawa Way
San Jose, CA 95130
(408) 364-1124
www.eragraphics.com

Kodomo No Kao Co., Ltd.
4-6-2 Higashinakano Nakano
Tokyo, Japan
011-81-3-3360-9806

Out West
P.O. Box 6921
Apache Junction, AZ 85278
(480) 288-5800

Personal Stamp Exchange
360 Sutton Place
Santa Rosa, CA 95407
(707) 588-8058
www.homesweetzone.com

Print Blocks
1/81 Bishop Street
Kelvin Grove
Brisbane Qld 4059
Australia
(07) 3356 7933
E-mail: printb@powerup.com.au

Rubber Stampede
2550 Pellissier Place
Whittier, CA 90601
(800) 623-8386

Other supplies

Artistic Wire Ltd.
752 N. Larch Avenue
Elmhurst, IL 60126
(630) 530-7567
www.artisticwire.com
E-mail: artwire97@aol.com
permanent colored copper wire

Chemtek
(888) 871-8100
www.chemtek.com
instant metallic finishes

Clearsnap, Inc.
Box 98
Anacortes, WA 98221
(800) 448-4862
(360) 293-6634
www.clearsnap.com
E-mail: contact@clearsnap.com
inkpads, stamps and accessories

Fascinating Folds
P.O. Box 10070
Glendale, AZ 85318
(800) 968-2418
(602) 375-9908
www.fascinating-folds.com
paper products and kits

Lenderink Technologies
P.O. Box 310
Belmont, MI 49306
(616) 887-8257
paper wood

Ranger Industries
15 Park Road
Tinton Falls, NJ 07724
(732) 389-3535
www.rangerink.com
inks and accessories

ScottiCrafts
Mount Vernon, NY
www.scotticrafts.com
UltimateBond and accessories

SDK Distributors
P.O. Box 421
Marlboro, NJ 07746
(800) 546-8641
E-mail: bonecraft9@aol.com

Index

get creative with *rubber stamps!*

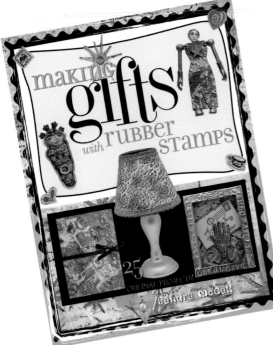

Make unique, expressive gifts with rubber stamps in combination with mixed media such as polymer clay, shrink plastic, handmade paper and more. Each project demonstrates a specific technique, then goes on to include stunning examples of how each technique can be combined or refined to produce a sophisticated piece of art.

1-58180-081-9, paperback, 128 pages

MaryJo McGraw takes stamping a step further! Inside, she'll show you fun, fast and easy ways to create fancier greeting cards, cooler note cards and prettier invitations. Includes more than 30 easy-to-follow, step-by-step projects that show you how to mix and match techniques for truly original results!

0-89134-878-6, paperback, 128 pages

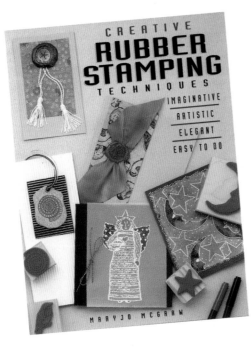

Discover great new tricks for creating extra-special greeting cards! Pick up your stamp, follow along with the illustrated, step-by-step directions inside, and ta da!—you'll amaze everyone (including yourself!) with your beautiful and original creations.

0-89134-979-0, paperback, 128 pages